A LETTER THAT LED TO FAME

Robert Peprah-Gyamfi

Kiddy Kiddy Books

Illustrated by: Jessica Otabil

Published by Kiddy Kiddy Books
www.kiddykiddybooks.com
email: info@kiddykiddybooks.com

ISBN: 978-1-913285-11-1

KIDDY KIDDY BOOKS SERIES No. 16

A LETTER THAT LED TO FAME

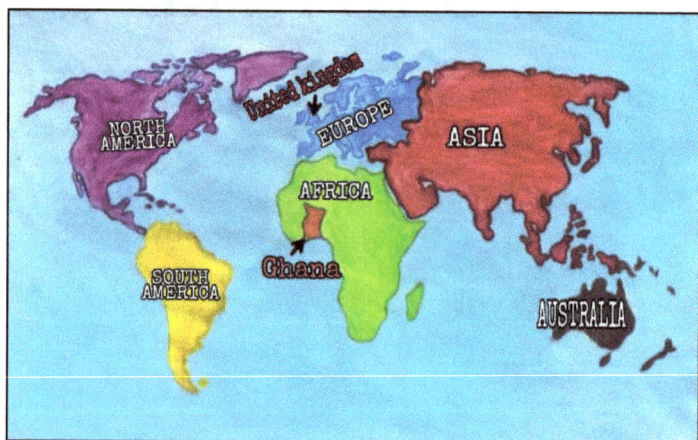

A LETTER THAT LED TO FAME is part of the KIDDY KIDDY Books Series. The series follows the life of Kofi Mensah, a little boy growing up in Kookookrom, a tiny village in Ghana, West Africa.

Let me tell you about Kofi Mensah. He is nine years old. He lives in a little village in Ghana, in West Africa. The village is called Kookookrom which means Cocoa Settlement.

Kofi is in Year 4 at primary school. There is no school in Kofi's village. Kofi and other children of the village have to walk to Mangokrom, the next village, to attend school. Mangokrom is two miles (three kilometres) to the north of Kookookrom. Mangokrom means Mango Settlement.

Residents of Kookookrom are poor. None of them is able to purchase a pair of sandals or shoes for their children. Because of this all the children of the village walk to school on their bare feet.

One day as Kofi and two of his friends were walking back home from school they met four men carrying someone on a stretcher. The men were heading in the direction they were coming from.

Kofi wondered what was the matter with the person on the stretcher. He engaged one of the men in conversation.

"Excuse me, Sir, what is wrong with your friend?"

"He was bitten on the right leg by a cobra whilst working on his cocoa farm. The cobra is a very dangerous snake. Its venom can lead to death in its victims. We are very concerned for our friend. We are carrying him to hospital. We are hoping and praying he makes it to the hospital alive."

"But there is no clinic around here! I grew up here so I know the nearest one is at Makokrom."

"Yes, we are taking him to the Makokrom Roman Catholic Hospital."

"But that is very far away. My parents took me there last year. I was suffering from chickenpox!"

"Well, we have no choice. As you are also aware, that is the nearest hospital."

"How will you get there?"

"We are hoping and praying a vehicle will pass by and give us a lift."

"Unfortunately, that is not likely."

"Why not?"

"We walk along this road to school and back, Mondays to Fridays. It is approaching 5pm. At this time of the day, hardly any vehicles pass by."

"Well, we are hoping for a miracle. There is nothing else we can do. So goodbye little one, we have to continue our walk."

"We wish you all the best," the three little pupils said as if with a single voice.

As Kofi continued his walk home, he kept thinking of the seriously ill patient. It reminded him of the case of one of the residents of their village. He too was bitten by a snake as he worked on his farm. He was carried from the farm to the village to await a vehicle to take him to hospital. As they waited, sadly, he died. Kofi hoped and prayed that the man on the stretcher would live and not die.

On his arrival home, Kofi's mother noticed he was not as cheerful as he usually was.

"What is the matter with you?" she inquired.

Kofi told her about the sick man being carried to hospital by the four men.

"That is really sad," his mother began. "A young person like you will find it particularly upsetting. I grew up in this community. Sadly, I have witnessed several such upsetting situations in my life so I have become used to them."

"Surely we cannot allow such tragic situations to continue," Kofi said. "We have to do something to improve the situation."

"What can we do, Kofi my dear? We live in a little village. We are all poor farmers. Nobody here, apart from you little ones, can read and write."

"I cannot just sweep the matter under the carpet!"

"What can you do to change the situation, my dear?"

"I am thinking about it. We have been taught in school to develop the habit of problem-solving. Put another way, we are to do what we can to find answers to problems and difficulties that come our way in life."

"Well, I wish you all the best, my dear!"

Kofi kept thinking about the sick man. The scene of the pitiful faces of the sick man and the four men carrying him kept coming back to him. He became so sad he lost his appetite. When his dinner was served to him, he just sat down looking at the meal instead of eating it. Kofi's mother took note of the situation.

"Kofi, eat your dinner!" she urged him.

"I am not hungry," he replied.

"Kofi, you walked two miles home from school. You must be hungry!"

After his mother kept urging him to eat his meal, Kofi began to do so. In the end he was able to eat only half of his plate.

Shortly after dinner he walked up to his mother and began:

"Mama, have you got some money to spare, please?"

"What for?"

"To purchase a pen and paper."

"Pen and paper?"

"Yes, Ma'am."

"But I thought the Government supplies them for free. That is what our MP told us when he visited us not long ago."

"We are yet to receive anything. Our teacher told us to expect them next week."

"What do you need the pen and paper for?"

"I want to write to our President."

"You want to write to our President?"

"Yes, you heard me right!"

"You must be dreaming!" exclaimed his father who was following the conversation.

"No, I am not," Kofi stated firmly.

"Why do you want to write to the President?" his father asked.

"I want to inform him about my meeting with the four men carrying the sick man to hospital."

"Boy, the President is too busy to be interested in such matters."

"No, he should not be too busy to concern himself with the problems of the citizens of the country. That's is what he was elected to do!"

"I don't want to argue with you, my little one. Just let me know what exactly it is you intend telling him."

"Okay, here we go:

"I will begin the letter by describing the incident of the sick man being carried to hospital. I will continue by informing him that the nearest hospital to our village is twenty miles away.. I will let him know that due to the long distance to hospital, residents often die from snake bites, during childbirth and from other illnesses before they get to the hospital. I will end my letter by pleading with him to build a hospital in the area to serve ourselves and residents of the other surrounding villages."

"Good luck with your effort, Kofi," his mother smiled. "We have been doing exactly that for years. We have on several occasions appealed to our MP not only to put up a hospital for us, but also to repair the poor road—and nothing has changed."

"We learnt at school today the following: 'If at first you don't succeed, try, try, try again!'"

"You are a real dreamer, Kofi!" his mother remarked.

"Our teacher told us the following a few days ago: 'It is better to dream, not small dreams, but big dreams!'"

"What else have you learnt?" asked his father.

"We were taught today that in life one should never get tired of fighting for good causes!"

"Enough of the big ideas and thoughts, Kofi!" said his mother, still smiling while she reached for her handbag. "Here you are; take these last few coins in my purse!" She dropped a few coins from her wallet into his hands.

Moments later, Kofi was on his way to the little corner shop in the centre of the village—the only one of its kind in the little settlement.

He returned a few minutes later holding two sheets of paper and a pen.

Kofi had to hurry up. It was getting dark. He still had to do his homework and complete the President's letter before the fall of darkness. There was no electricity in the village. If it turned dark before he got the job done, he would have to make use of a kerosene lamp. He hated doing his homework with that source of light because of the foul-smelling fumes it blew into the air.

Kofi soon got to work.

First, he completed his homework for the day. Next, he turned his attention to the President's letter.

Below is what he wrote:

Dear Mr President,

I hope you are doing fine.

My name is Kofi Mensah. I am nine years old. I am in Year 4 at primary school.

I am contacting you to report an incident I witnessed whilst walking home from school today.

As I walked home from school with my two friends, we met four men carrying a man who had been bitten by a snake whilst working on his farm. They were hoping for a vehicle to take him to hospital. For your information, the nearest hospital is twenty miles away from where we met them.

We have learnt in school that those bitten by snakes require immediate medical attention. Sadly, that was not the case in this instance.

Our ways parted, so I do not know what happened to him. My fear is that he might have died before getting to the hospital.

As I just mentioned, the nearest hospital serving our area is twenty miles away. The road serving the area is also very poor. As a result of the poor road and the long distance to hospital, residents often die from emergencies such as snake bites, deep cut wounds, childbirth, etc, before they can receive medical attention.

To improve the healthcare provision of our village and the surrounding communities, I am humbly appealing to you to construct, without delay, a hospital for our community.

Thank you very much for your time.

Yours faithfully,
Kofi Mensah

Kofi placed the letter in the envelope, sealed it and addressed it to the President. Soon he realised he had no money to buy the stamps for the postage.

'Mama gave me the money for the pen and paper,' he said to himself, and concluded: 'It is now Papa's turn to give me money for the postage.'

Soon he was facing his father.

"Papa, Mama gave me money for the paper and pen. Can you please give me money for the stamps?"

"My goodness, this young boy will want to take the very last penny from me!"

"Please Papa, help me! We learnt at school that "He who says A, must say B'."

"What does it me?"

"Well Miss Osei, our teacher explained it as follows:

If you say or do one thing, you must be prepared to do what logically follows. In this case, I have been given money for the pen and paper, so I should also be given money for the stamps."

"Oh boy, you are learning great things at school. Still I do not agree with you completely on the matter."

"Why not?"

"It was not myself who said the A to start with. It was rather your mother, so you have to ask her to say the B as well!"

"Friend, just give him something," Kofi's mother urged her husband. "Who knows what will come out of his efforts."

"Okay, here you are, boy." Kofi's father opened his wallet and dropped a few coins into the hands of his little boy.

"Thanks to both of you for your help!" Kofi shouted at the top of his voice. For a while he kept hopping and jumping around in delight.

There was no post office in the village; the nearest was at Mangokrom.

Kofi took the letter along with him to school the next day. During the lunch break he walked to the post office. He went alone. He did not want any of his friends to know about his plans.

When he presented the letter at the post office, the postman was very surprised to read the address on the envelope.

"A letter for our President?" he asked Kofi.

Kofi could read the surprise written on his face.

"Yes, please," he replied calmly.

"Who wrote it?"

"Why do you want to know?"

"Ach, it is just me, the grey-haired old man, being inquisitive."

"Myself," Kofi replied, still remaining calm.

"*You*, writing to the President of the country!"

"What is wrong with that?"

"Hmm!"

"You have not answered my question!"

"Well, I thought it was only well-placed members of society who are expected to write to the President."

"I am afraid I don't agree with you on the matter. The President is there to serve everyone, including a poor farmer's son from Kookookrom!"

"So you are from Kookookrom?"

"Yes indeed."

"And you walk from your village to attend school every day?"

"Yes indeed."

"That is very stressful. I wish the Government could supply buses to convey you to and from school. Anyway, back to your letter. Since you are sending it to the President, I have to inspect it."

"Why?"

"To make sure there is no bomb hidden in it!"

"A bomb? Why should I conceal a bomb in it?"

"Unfortunately, we live in a world where some use force to achieve their goals. For security reasons therefore, we inspect all letters meant for our President."

"I believe in the power of argument; in the power of persuasion—not in force."

"Hey, little one, where did you learn such wisdom?"

"I read it in my school library."

"Really?"

"Yes indeed. Concerning your request to inspect the letter, I am not against it. I see a problem, though."

"What problem?"

"The problem of money. My parents gave me their last penny to buy the pen and paper as well as pay for the postage. If this envelope becomes damaged after you have opened the letter, I don't have any money left for another envelope."

"Oh, I get your point. No worries. I will take care of that."

Quickly the postmaster opened and inspected the envelope.

Happily, the envelope was not damaged. Kofi then paid for the postage and left the letter with the postman.

"Goodbye, Sir!"

"Goodbye, my dear. I enjoyed your company. You are welcome to visit for a chat whenever you are free."

* * *

For a long while Kofi did not hear anything from the President. Indeed, he thought either the letter went missing on the way or the President was not interested in writing a reply.

Then came Independence Day of Ghana. It is a tradition in the country for the President to speak to the whole country at seven o'clock in the evening on Independence Day.

Kofi and his family gathered around their little radio set to listen to the President's address to the nation.

In the middle of the speech, Kofi felt tired and began to nod off.

"Hey, Kofi, don't sleep. You have got to pay attention to our President," said his mother, shaking him gently as she spoke.

Kofi woke up and began paying attention to the President.

What perfect timing it was! Just as Kofi began paying attention to the speech, the President spoke the following words:

"We need individuals with a strong sense of duty, citizens who are inclined to fight for what is right. I want in particular to cite the case of a little boy, Kofi Mensah, from the little village of Kookookrom. Before I became involved with his case, I had no idea where the little village is located. Now I know; it is located in the Birim North District of the Eastern Region.

"One day whilst returning home from school Kofi saw a pathetic scene—of four individuals carrying someone who had been bitten by a snake on a stretcher.

"Kofi felt a deep sense of duty, the urge to do something about the situation.

"He considered it his civic duty to bring the matter to the attention of the President and plead with him to build a hospital in his area to improve the healthcare provision of the area.

"Fellow countrymen and countrywomen, let us pause for a moment and think about the matter! A nine-year-old boy taking it upon himself to write to the President of his country to draw his attention to what no doubt is a very sad state of affairs. These are the kind of citizens needed for our nation-building efforts.

"Little Kofi Mensah, if you happen to be listening to this speech, I want to announce that in the first place you have been awarded an Independence Day Medal.

"Arrangements will be made for a state car to fetch you and your parents, in addition to two individuals of your own choice, to attend the Independence Day Award Ceremony at the presidential palace this weekend!

"Secondly, I have directed that a district hospital should be constructed in your area as soon as possible. I will personally be present to cut the tape to mark the beginning of work on the hospital."

As might be expected, Kofi was greatly flabbergasted! He thought he was in a dream and not in the real world! Never in his best of dreams could he ever have imagined he would be so honoured.

The rest of the family joined Kofi in celebrating the good news.

As promised by the President, a state vehicle was sent to pick up Kofi and members of his family for the Award Ceremony.

The colourful ceremony took place at the State House in Accra .

In time the hospital was also built, as promised.

The residents decided to name the hospital after Kofi. Kofi was a special guest at the official ceremony organised to announce the name to the public. As expected, Kofi felt very proud of the honour done to his name.

As he lay in bed that night, Kofi said to himself: "I am going to learn very hard at school so I can become a doctor one day and work at the Kofi Mensah Hospital."

Look out for more exciting stories about the life experiences of Kofi Mensah, the little boy from Kookokoo, in Ghana, West Africa.

Glossary

Award Ceremony — When medals or awards are presented.

Chickenpox — A viral infection characterised by red blisters all over the body.

Citizen — A person who has rights in the country they live in because they were born there or because of being given rights after having lived there for several years.

Civic duty — Responsibility expected from all members of a society.

Flabbergasted — Really surprised or astonished.

Ghana — A country in West Africa.

Independence Day — A day celebrating the anniversary of a nation's independence.

Kerosene — Paraffin used in homes in lamps and for heating.

Kofi — Boy's name, meaning born on a Friday.

Birim ND — Name of a district in the Eastern Region of Ghana.

Kookookrom	Name of Kofi's village, meaning Cocoa Settlement.
Long break	Lunchtime at school.
Mangokrom	A village 3km to the north of Kookookrom. Means mango village.
Mensah	If parents give birth to a boy, to be followed directly by a boy and yet another boy, the third boy is called Mensah.
MP	Member of Parliament.
Pesewa	Name of the small unit of currency (coins) in Ghana.
President	The man voted by the people to lead them.
Problem-solving	Trying to find answers to problems and difficulties

ABOUT THE AUTHOR

Dr. Robert Peprah-Gyamfi grew up in Mpintimpi, a little village in Ghana, West Africa.

He faced many challenges growing up in that impoverished village. Despite the challenging living conditions he faced growing up in that impoverished village, he later made it to the Hannover Medical School in Germany, where he qualified as a doctor in 1992.

Robert now works part -time as a doctor and spends the rest of his time writing. Indeed, he has been a passionate storyteller from a young age. He started his first novel as a teenager, but could not however finish his work due to lack of resources.

Robert, who regards himself as citizen of the Global Village, is currently resident in the UK.

To connect with him please visit: www.kiddykiddybooks.com